In the Shadow
of the Globe

To Gail —
All the best!

In the Shadow
of the Globe

a poetic narrative in ten acts

by Michelle Cameron

Michelle Cameron

edited by Beverly A. Jackson

Lit Pot Press, Inc.
Fallbrook, California

In the Shadow of the Globe

Cover art and layout design by Eileen Murray © 2003; back cover photo by Peter Vidor © 2003

First U.S. Edition
Published by Lit Pot Press, Inc., Fallbrook, CA. USA
Printed in Canada by Stride Print Services

Library of Congress Cataloging in Publication Data

Cameron, Michelle
        In the Shadow of the Globe - First Edition 2003

1 Poetry
Library of Congress Control Number: 2003112626
ISBN 0-9743919-2-1

Lit Pot Press, Inc.
3909 Reche Rd. Ste. #132
Fallbrook, CA 92028

For Steve, Geoff, and Alex
who taught me passion, courage, and perservance

Contents

At the Globe Theatre for a Limited Engagement!

 **ooden O:
the Burbage Legacy**

} How one family ruled London theatre for two generations — their passion for acting, for building, and for the box office takings.

P r i n c i p a l   A c t o r s
James Burbage, *actor, builder of London's first Theatre*
Cuthbert Burbage, *James' oldest son, company manager*
Richard Burbage, *James' youngest son, leading actor*
Mary Burbage, *James' youngest daughter*
William Shakespeare, *actor*
Peter Street, *master carpenter*

a n d   a l s o
James Brayne, *James Burbage's brother in law*
Mistress Brayne, *James Burbage's sister*

My Father, Dreamer, Builder

MARY BURBAGE:

1.

When he wanted to hurt me,
Father would call me accident child,
the one unwanted,
the one who came too late,
the one who killed her mother.

2.

There were nights —
a few at least —
when he'd hold us, all three,
my brothers, Cuthbert, Richard,
together with me, tiny Mary,
and talk of his travels:
how he'd sleep
in poor taverns,
knife under his pillow
or in a hayfield
under the bowl
of spilled stars,
actors playing innyards
and town squares,
payment scant,
supper a few potatoes,
a cup of sack.

He'd tell us of the great theatres
of Athens, Rome, Byzantium,
how the mighty would sit
under a blue Mediterranean sky,
pay in antique coin
chiseled with profiles of Emperors,
how the ancients
would play the lost tragedies,
booming voices echoing off
chalky foothills.

Someday, he vowed to us —
we three rapt in the warmth
of his voice, his attention —
someday, London, too,
would have a Theatre of its own

and he would build it.

3.
my baby days:
all hammer song
and walking shod —

too easy to stumble
over splintering beams,
trip on mislaid tools,

and yet, there was magic:
shells of buildings
rising, shaped
by my father's hand,

his voice throaty, deep,
drama in his movement,
in his commands, his excuses,

a man too used
to woo audiences
to love easily,
every inch of him
built for applause.

4.
Under Father's splintering eye
I learned to move, fast, fast,
bring what was wanted,
be quiet, watchful,
wait for love.

Shakespeare Seeks a Position

MARY BURBAGE:
Thinking himself concealed
by the great oak,
he spit in his hand,
smoothed back his hair,
tugged at his doublet,
twisting it, to lie flat,

made himself walk up
the smooth stone to the door,
slipped off,
stepped back,

and knocked.

I flew to answer,
the fleet desire of my steps
surprising me.

I liked his eyes: blue,
nervous, kind.

Father spoke to him.
I hovered near,
listening all afternoon:
a jumble of horse-holding,

soldiering, ships at faraway ports,
rustic schools, father a glover,
an absolute ache for the stage.

(And, he said, he wrote
the odd tale here and there —
was encouraged by Kit Marlowe,
was certain he could produce a play or two
had we need for it.)

He never mentioned a wife.

Not that it would have mattered,
not to Father, who took him off
to meet the rest of the Company,
brushing by me, as if I were not there.

Breaking the Lease

MARY BURBAGE:

Before we left the cemetery,
dirt piled high above my father,
Cuthbert barked orders —
stop moaning, sister, hie home,
lay out food for our guests.

Years of scurrying
to one set of commands
inured me to another —

by the time the actors trooped inside,
shivering in capes and cloaks,
a snapping fire in the grate
ham, cheese, bread neatly laid
up on the table —
my misery laid there, too,
for them to drink and eat.

Before they downed second winecup,
they shrugged Father's memory aside
for other matters:

We cannot afford the new terms of the lease,
said Cuthbert, puffed up
sudden man-about-the-house,
I know an inexpensive plot,
but we cannot afford timber to build, either.

Some banter about knocking heads for sense,
making do with pitch and wattle,

then young Shakespeare leaned forward, spoke:
'Tis our lumber in the Theatre, is it not?
What stops us removing it to less expensive ground?

The simple beauty of it stole upon their faces,
grins rising as the moon upon a starstruck sky.

Near dark, night closing in too early,
I hunched over plates, mourning father,
clutching my pain in cutlery,
when he took my dirty cargo, set it aside:

I meant to bid you sorry for your loss earlier —
he put lips to my ear almost,
warmth upon my cheek a spring caress.

I stood still under his blue gaze
the simple beauty of him
reflected in collected tears,
something stirred within me,
his kindness refracted
like a pond disturbed,

a crystalline gripping,
new clutch, new growth,
new thrusting of life shoot.

Richard Mourns His Father

RICHARD BURBAGE:

The day I first played
for the Queen, my father sat,
smoking a pipe before the fire,
playing every scene within his head.

He knew my lines,
the very heart,
and enough of the rest
to throw his arms around them
all that proud afternoon.

Burbage Brothers

CUTHBERT BURBAGE:

    When we were boys,
I'd tuck a tiny Richard under bedclothes,
tell him stories of Spanish marauders
how Catholics would catch him,
burn him at the stake.

    He'd cry himself to sleep,
fearing his dreams, my revenge on him
for being Father's favourite,
bright, sparkling cherub,
successor to the Burbage family fame.

    Me, I was dull. Father would rage,
trying sharp words to recarve me in his image.
I was stolid, never gave way to tears
the way fearful wee Dick did.

    But, afterward, my chest would burn for hours.

    Father quarreled building London's first Theatre,
he and Uncle Brayne barraging one other
with the cutting edge of wit.
I'd play step-and-fetch-it,
bringing planks of wood and cut charcoal

for them to blunt out plans, smudging a building
in smeared grey under their blackening fingers.
Father approved when I saved on costs,

but it was still Dick he'd smile on later at dinner —

and the day young Richard ran full tilt
at my uncle's widow, brandishing a broom,
to keep her fingers from the till, now that —
that — was a brave deed in my father's eyes!
One might imagine his stalwart lad
had just braved the Spanish Armada,
come ashore off their flotilla,
breast armour and feathered helmet gleaming,
the way my father preened and praised!

Well, Father died content, that's certain,
seeing his young hero made much of,
applauded by Her Very Royal Self
all her courtiers and ladies
and we brought the planks
of Father's famous Theatre to Southwark,
our last tribute —

(and incidentally,
to save on cost of lumber) —

and under their sheltering beams
I push back the burning in my chest,
count out, daily,
a full quarter of the takings,
all mine to do with
whatever I might wish.

Wooden O

INSTRUCTIONS FROM CUTHBERT BURBAGE
TO PETER STREET, MASTER CARPENTER,
TO CONSTRUCT THE GLOBE THEATRE:

Here is where
the actors will prance,
they will hold out their arms
and sing, will love and cavort,
dance, plot, fight,
die,

then live again.

Here, smooth planks rising
from the ground:
a space for hundreds —
or at least, their ghosts —

for castles
and Venetian moats,
dungeons, battlefields,
intimate lovers
wistfully waiting
on balconies

(up there,
above a door,
build a balcony)

and mark well
places enough
for exits and entrances,
for confusion,
for comic hiding in corners,
the dozen mishaps that happen
in love's unsmooth courses,
or tragically,
as men will skulk, unseen,
behind a deep, rich arras,
to hear aught
they should not know,

and don't forget the flag pole
on the half-roof.
We'll fly our colors there
every afternoon,

our flag, gay with the Globe
in universe's center,
as soon shall we be,
to London
and our entire world.

The Perils of Bankside, Site of Our New Globe Theatre

WILLIAM SHAKESPEARE:

The whores sleep till noon,
but are lined up enticing,
angling for our apprentices
when they leave rehearsal.

I tell the lads of French pox,
how scabs and pus grip their balls,
what it's like to strain
over scorched flux piss,

but they grin at me, little cocks,
chests crowded with pride
that I need to scare them,

eyes all carnival fascination
at garish painted faces
purpling of lips, rouge about nipples
offered freely from gaping flimsy cloth —

so much to grab and buy! I want to snatch
them, wide-eyed innocents, by scabbed elbows,
propel them, stiff legged,
past strumpets flaunting,
push them into the shade of the great Clink,

point at barred windows, explain how these
gaoled men wandered, thoughtless,
through Southwark alleys,
spending more coin than found in pocket:
in drink, in dice, in whores,
spun into the shadow of their desires, until,
caught sick, bruised, wretched,
their day waned to nothing more
than the faintest bar of light
on a stony, rat-infested floor.

Writing Romances

MARY BURBAGE:

He has notions, this William,
whom I watch skritch-scratching
words in a torrent of inspiration —

words that sing, all birdsong, forest shadings,
him their lark, chest swelling, wooing a world
that holds me, ennested, spellbound —

around him, Bankside squalor,
fellows drinking, catcalling, making merry,
but he, abstracted, pays heed only to his quill,
to romances that snare me breathless
when I sneak and read them.

Each morning, I choose my hairpiece,
my apron, neat bands about my sleeves,
watch for his empty plate, his tepid ale,
do what I can to replenish his musings —

he rewarding me with that blue glint
wink, kind smile, a glance up, down,
when I arrive, when I leave.

My brothers speak, bewildered,
of this Anne Hathaway his wife
— older than him, they say,
three children, one dead, they say.

None of it matters when I read his lines,
nay, nor when he enters a room
and my breath comes
prickly in my chest, my legs,
warm glowing in my cheeks and,
(yes I must admit),
burning red hot elsewhere.

The acclaimed Globe Theatre production of

Pride & Passion

Can William Shakespeare overcome a rustic past to become a respected member of noble London? Will his words woo his way to the bed of the mysterious, sensual Dark Lady?

Principal Players

William Shakespeare, poet, playwright, actor
Henry Southampton, Earl of Wriothesley,
    Shakespeare's patron
The Mysterious Dark Lady
Anne Hathaway, Shakespeare's wife
Mary Burbage, sister to the Burbage brothers,
    principal owners of the Globe Company

and also

Susanna Shakespeare, Shakespeare's oldest daughter
Judith Shakespeare, Shakespeare's youngest daughter
Hamnet Shakespeare, Judith's twin,
    Shakespeare's deceased son

For My Patron, Lord Southampton

WILLIAM SHAKESPEARE:
He of the golden curls,
the golden life,
smiles upon me
and I am blind —

blind but not dumb.
I take my pen
in his praise,

his circle opening
tight clasps
to cinch me inside
as plaything
no less valuable
than hounds or horse —
but perhaps no more —

pointed to as corner poet
haunting nooks unwanted,
watching them,
their gilded lives
trailing past.

I am here to curry favor —
amuse them with puffery and praise:

Henry Southampton,
what I have done is yours;
what I have to do is yours;
being part in all I have,
devoted yours*

you take from me
some space of time
my eyes,
but grant me
fairest freedom
for my tongue.

* Shakespeare's dedication in *The Rape of Lucrece*.

Lust in Action

WILLIAM SHAKESPEARE:

Suddenly, making use of conceits
borrowed from centuries of constraint —
courtly verses, bowing,
waving a fan —
all, all seem senseless
beside her liquid lips,
the tangle of her hair
wild down her back,
the curve of her lithe body,
seen faintly through stiff guardians
of corset and petticoat!

Seeing the Dark Lady
in Southampton's marble halls,
sipping from a silver cup,
nibbling dainty cakes,

I want to roar,
return her to a barbarian past,
sweep her onto a maddened steed,
ride off, possess her —
willing, unwilling, it matters not —
in some wretched hut, her limbs splayed,
open to me, the fire blazing
in our thrust and parry!

But I batten down
the rising of my lust,
scrape, bow,
whisper nothings
in her ear, seek only
to do what pleases.

Anything else
awakens her disdain,
makes her turn from me,
a country oaf, farm girl's husband,
theatrical clown,
not fit to touch the fingers
of her soft white hand.

At night, by the fire,
I read old Wyatt
and feel his fury
at his playful, fickle mistress,
the one who maddened him,
whispering *yes, yes, no.*

Yet she reads my verse
and blushes, turns away,
hides herself and her confusion
behind a hasty fan.

The words come
ready to my quill.
Let me slip them
like a sleeping draught
in her cordial cup,
making her drowsy,
pliant to my seductive touch.

Remembering Avon's Haystacks

WILLIAM SHAKESPEARE:

At sixteen, all I thought of
was this pole between my legs
and where I could stick it.

It's a springtide sickness,
sap rising, nectar
aching to be sucked.

Her breasts high and proud,
my palms itched for them,
and for her moan and the slow,
sure surge of her generous hips.

They've always wanted to know
how I feel toward her, this wife
I left behind, waiting,
watering her impatience
with buckets from Avon's streams.

The young ones think there's
some mystery, something beyond
her hairs rising up, strand by strand
from her matted nest,

beyond the urge to plunge
past her farmyard arms
to ecstasy.

My Husband

ANNE HATHAWAY:

    The garden bloomed on your birthday,
    April twenty-third,
    and Judith gathered up
    the dancing buds and laughed.

    With the spring, there are renewed fears,
    here, of plague — we keep isolated,
    hope to pray ourselves safe.

    (Oh, William, can you not write
    us more? Must all your words
    live and die onstage?)

    I planted a new sapling
    in the corner near the spruce —
    where Hamnet used to play.

    When the wind blows,
    I imagine him in the boughs
    laughing down at me.

    The money you sent, my dear,
    was more than enough
    for this fair weather season —

I bought Susanna cloth for a spring dress,
and your father fashioned Judith
a new set of Sunday gloves —

they're growing so, like the honeysuckle
that climbs the side of the dovecot,
now —

(Oh, William, if they close the Globe
for plague, will you summer at home?
You'd please us, my dear, to spend
a little time with us who miss you so.

I promise we will let you write.)

Dark Lady

HER SERVANT SPEAKS:
    Mid-morning, and my lady drowses,
    smiling at a memory of the night
    and the soft blandishments of the poet
    who shared her covers for awhile.

    There are no lovers like poets,
    she whispered — only yesterday?
    — to Katrice, who raised one gilt eyebrow
    and leaned in, to catch recountings
    of his languid and lingual attentions
    to her dun flanks, dark hair,
    the eyes he claimed sparked black lightning.

    Married? Oh, yes, to some drab
    buried in the country —
    something, too, about a son lost —

    but he doesn't waste their too-few hours
    in complaints, except when she is late
    to meet him at their favorite spot
    by Southampton's roses,
    near the misting fountains

— some afternoons so remiss,
he'll have scattered a deep red cushion
upon the stone ledge, counting minutes
plucking petals, showering her, half joking,
when she finally arrives, only to say she's late
and must already leave him.

It won't last, of course. He'll tire, or she will.
But, oh, for now,
she can still taste his words upon her lips,
his eyes shaping her
into lines, stanzas, sonnets, couplets, verse.

Shakespeare in Guise of Courtier

MARY BURBAGE:

My songbird, lark,
hurries all unlike him,
reeking of some scent
he hopes will mask his labor,
three hours upon the stage.

The others laugh,
call him *Monseiur Le Beau*
of the mushroom cap,
beg him to show them
the trick of making a proper bow
in the halls of noblemen.

He shrugs, good natured,
ignores their gibes,
finds time to perfect
young Samuel's dancing,
slips Nick Tooley a penny
to buy sweet buns
for apprentices and stagehands,

sits writing sonnets by the hour,
crumples his wife's screeds,
uses their backs for poems
to woo his splendid mistress.

The man confounds me:

I look to him for what is most foolish
and find something within me melts.

To Every Man His Part — and Woman, Too

✦ Go backstage at the Globe Theatre
✦ For Rivalry and Good Fellowship!

Principal Actors:
Mary Burbage, sister to the Burbage brothers
Ralph Crane, official Globe scribe
Nicholas Tooley, apprentice
Alexander Cooke, apprentice

Also featuring:
Ben Jonson, writer
Tom Kyd, writer
Will Slye, hireling
Will Kempe, clown
Cuthbert Burbage, theatre manager
Philip Henslowe, rival theatre manager
Scribbler of the rival theatre company
Maidservant
Two gawky lads

Playing This Month Only
at the Globe Theatre in Bankside!

Backstage

MARY BURBAGE:

They call *Mary Mary*
and I come running

a stitch needed here
find the broom
find the boys
find the shoes

I count the hours
by how many calls
I've heard
Mary Mary

count the takings
buy the bread
wipe the tear

Mary Mary
the apprentices laugh
don't marry Mary
what would we do
without Mary

my feet trip lightly
into the dark corners
backstage

my day a chorus
singing my name

Company Scribe, Script Safekeeper

RALPH CRANE:

Happy I am to live in a time
when every man's spelling
is every man's choice!

The pad on my thumb's base
has thickened with the years;
my eyes lined, red-rimmed from peering
into the hearts of men who write.

I identify a playwright
by his loops and curlicues:
can see old Tom Kyd
has sharpened his sputtering quill,
when Jonson works at night
from his splatter of spilled tallow
across the page.

They know me, too,
by the chain wrapped nightly
round the safebox,
thick iron key hugged to my chest,
clasped tighter than a mistress,
its caress marking me with indent
at cock's crow.

Transcribed, the words
dance before me — glittering,
sure-footed devils, daring me
to chase them onto the page.

I stand too close, sometimes,
to the cannon's maw of art,
burned by fire, ash, explosion,
gaping wide-mouthed,
as the molten ball
goes shrieking off.

Our Rival, Philip Henslowe

MARY BURBAGE:

We have rivals, of course,
but none so crafty as Philip Henslowe,
owner of brothels,
bear baiting rings, a lucrative practice

in usury, a man of many ventures,
not inspired by love of the stage,
theatres merely another way
to gather up sweet clink of coin.

Cuthbert says again: *Henslowe
singlehanded is creating
a ripe underbelly of vice
next door to our Globe.*

I hear something in Cuthbert's voice
as he repeats himself —
something in his voice
makes me flinch.

Behind the Barrow

NICHOLAS TOOLEY, APPRENTICE:

The others love the hunt —
see them, panting and alive,
whipping their staves about them,
waiting for prey.

Me, I'd rather be learning lines,
or sweeping the stage, or hanging
about to catch a morsel of gossip,
a bit of news.

Henslowe's boys are a raucous bunch,
bigger than us, nastier, too,

and who's to say, really,
that it's them who've been ripping
our playbills from the posts?

Do we have proof? What is this
but flesh given to wild imaginings
— the posters gone
and angry accusations fly through air,
and it's Henslowe, or rather,
Henslowe's boys have done it —

hot anger and spite,
calls for revenge —
and here we are, cudgels in hand,
waiting since dawn.

Scribbler!

ALEXANDER COOKE, APPRENTICE:
What did he think,
that old man —
that no one would see him?

Writing out our every word,
gold falling from our lips,
stealing lines like pennies —

could you blame us
for being, well, harsh with him?

Aye, yes, 'tis true we kicked him,
tore his pages, every one,
hit him about the face,
in the chest, about his shins,

carried him above a jeering crowd
which parted for us, a Red Sea
before Moses, all the way to the door.

Were we gentle? No.
But what did he think,
old creature of Devil Henslowe,
he'd have at our hands,
if not dire thrashing —

yes, we had at him,
hearts rising, triumphant,
as he slunk away,
a beat dog, weeping,
creeping defeated on all fours.

My Lark, Our Fortune

MARY BURBAGE:

    At dinner, Cuthbert spoke of Henslowe —
well, to say spoke, bit him savage rather,
masticated as bloody meat, spit him out,
well gnawed, to the dogs — rivalry
so galling he painted Henslowe in horns and tail,
content with nothing less for him than hellfire,
convincing if I did not know him,
his neat suit, ruddy face, affable bow in church —

    and Richard, sharing supper, quaffed
the bitter dregs of conversation lightly —

    so much do Companies share, Dick said peaceably:
we have lads, as do they, we a stage, as do they,
we actors, fine swordsmen, musicians, dancers,
but they do rival us — in all corners
and all quarters, all but one.

    And together Dick and Cuthbert raised their cups
to toast my dear lark —
William, bard of the Globe!

    ours, all ours, they gloated, drinking deep.

Buying Clothes

ALEXANDER COOKE, APPRENTICE:

1.

The servants titter at me
here in the gutter —
think I'm a manikin
plopped in place
for their fingers to point to.

A wiry wench yanks me inside,
her arms whipcord,
fingers bodkins
piercing my ear,
pulling me down the halls —

I tell her: *I've been*
to daintier places than this —
think of the times I've played
the Queen's palace —

but she snorts and drags me,
grumbling of rustic boors,
unlicked cubs,
thrusting me, ungently,
into this small chamber,
chiding me to wait some more.

2.

The ropy one returns
with two chittering lads
hauling a chest of clothes.

It's what we want:
velvets, fur linings,
brocade cloth —

I'm careful, now, to find the flaws,
cluck loudly over unlapped seams,

curl my lip at stains
from some night's
excess food and drink.

3.

Who would believe a man a king
if he dressed in worsted?

We may have no other trappings —
our swords are wood,
the marble on our columns painted —

but we wear the clothes of nobility —
carry them better, I fair swear,
than nobility itself —

know how to drape the mantle,
drag the farthingale,
brandish the feathered cap!

4.
Clinking the pretty pieces
into that rope-hard claw,
I know some of our dickering
won't reach her ladyship or her lord

(let her filch,
for silver sticks
to my inner linings, too)

but I make her pay —
subtract a sum

for the hours spent in the gutter,
for her harsh words, my ear grabbed,
and for the spit I saw floating
in my single cup of ale.

To the Woman Who Mistook Me
for a Woman from the Back

ALEXANDER COOKE, APPRENTICE:
   No, I'm not. They expect me
   only to move the dress, to sway
   across the stage, wave a fan,
   gather my farthingale
   to one side as I sashay,
   say my lines in a piercing high falsetto,
   hide my deepening voice
   that plunges down as I grow tall.

   I've dressed as so many women, now:
   Portia, Rosalind, and Olivia,
   each quick witted,
   seeking safe harbor in this dangerous world,
   Cleopatra, Titania, Lady Macbeth,
   powerful, assured,
   foolish in grasping more
   than their hands could hold,
   Desdemona, Juliet, Regan,
   poor doomed waifs
   — but I've only dressed as them.

   Do not mistake me as having
   their womanly ambitions,
   seeking love in the wrong corners,
   or even in the right —

yet do not make of me
a villain, either — as do our preachers,
their Puritan morality
gatekeeper to bar me from heaven,
calling me sinner for parading onstage
in fine feathers, silks that mislead foolish girls,

who should, indeed, be home now,
baking or sewing or snaring a husband
— wherefore have you embarked
on keeping me here defending your mistake
of my identity?

Go on now.
I've doublet and hose waiting.
And an ale among my fellows after that.

Off, farewell.

Onstage, with Flower

ALEXANDER COOKE, APPRENTICE:
My job
at this moment
is to stand
stock still
and wait.

In a moment
Burbage will
drop the knife
with a clatter,

clutch his breast,
groan heartrendingly.

In another moment
there will be a shout
off stage —
loud enough
for a hundred horsemen;

hirelings will dash through
pretending to be
on horseback.

In the moment after that
an opposing force
stage right,
will swarm,
have at it
swords and knives
merry curses —

backstage
stagehands will bang
on pots and tureens
a mighty clatter,

bodies be strewn about
agonized cries,
wailings, moaning

then trumpets
heralding the entrance
of the King to give
his final benediction.

In a moment.

But right now,
I have this blasted flower
in my hand,

and I have to sigh,
look lovingly
into my dear
beloved's eyes

— as though
I didn't know
what could happen
in a moment,

the kind of disaster
that waits in the wings:

the unexpected
knife thrust,
viciousness
of horsemen,
the flower
trampled,
forgotten,
swept aside.

Love's Labor, Unachieved

The tragedy of
the unrealized ambition —
the star-crossed love that
can never be...

Principal Players

William Shakespeare, poet, playwright, lover

The Mysterious Dark Lady

Henry Southampton, Earl of Wriothesley

Anne Hathaway, Shakespeare's wife

Orange Girl, a girl of the streets

Mary Burbage, of the Globe Theatre

A theatrical triumph
at the Globe Theatre, Southwark
See it today!

Discarded

WILLIAM SHAKESPEARE:

Flinging me aside like last year's fashions,
she says she tires of my sighs,
my whispers, my importuning,
my sonnets,
my love.

Her laugh a silvery tinkle,
now cold and clanging,
freezing the blood
that still throbs and pools
at the sight of her.

She tells me our passion
was never more than dalliance,
smiles through rouged lips
that I — yokel, hireling,
ink-stained lackey —
might aspire to more
than a few privileged nights.

I see her putting that small hand
through Southampton's arm
as he leads her to dance.

I want to close my eyes,
blot out sight of her — and him.
But, somehow, my lids refuse me,
become fiery prongs of torture,
making me watch:
unblinking, red-rimmed,
seared.

Dismissed

WILLIAM SHAKESPEARE:

Southampton picks up the chicken thigh,
speaks around the best part of the meat,
eating quickly, tossing the rest
into a trencher under his seat
for this month's favored hound.

Not my wish,
but you must see,
dear fellow,
she can't turn around
without spying you —
you're her specter
at the feast,
that white face
haunting all her peace.

I said I'd have a word.

Southampton wipes tacky fingers on his lace,
snaps for more wine.

Complaint

FROM A LETTER BY ANNE HATHAWAY
TO WILLIAM SHAKESPEARE:

The harvest failed, Will,
the sun so close and hot
it seared the fields.

There's nothing left
but next year's seedlings
and the money you send —

and we need more.

Don't write to us of poetry,
playhouses, Southampton,
London, the court.

We can't eat your tales.

Orange Girl

AT CHEAPSIDE MARKET:
She holds an orange,
sniffs the flowers of Seville,
the heavy, lacy odor —
she's never tasted one.

She hands over hoarded coins,
clammy from being held
against narrow,
not-yet-budding breasts.

Seville! Even the name smells ripe,
sunny, unlike the gutters
of Cheapside!

Once, someone showed her
a black lace mantilla,
said Spanish ladies
are spiders,
weaving, weaving.

AT THE GLOBE THEATRE:

She moves through crowds,
smiling, waving,
selling oranges,

watching the stage
from one corner of her eye
she wants the part of Juliet
oh Romeo Romeo
she cries, silent,
her mouth an o of orbed fruit,
her globed wordlessness
timed precisely
with the call of the boy
draped in lacy garb

(she's seen the play three times this month)

oh to be in Mantua or Venice or Seville
and not here tromping through mud,
faint aroma of unpeeled orange
rising off her fingers,
lines beating, unheard,
from an untasted golden core.

74

Complaints

WILLIAM SHAKESPEARE:
The world views my poems
as baubles, playthings,
pretty if I were a lordling,
tricking and shifting at court —
which I am not.

(Which I will never be.)

When my Dark Lady loved me,
I could not stop the flow
of sonnets — I thought
they'd sweep us up,
their sway and power rich enough
to make us equal,

but she, careless, stuffed them
like so much stained lace
and stray pearl beads
into her casket of memories,

something to pull out
on a rainy day,
instead of riding to hounds.

They're starving, in Stratford,
Anne and the girls —
if my boy had lived,
he'd be starving, too.

Southampton, playing the patron's part,
tosses me gold for a poem,
or laughs and sharpens his wit
on it, and thinks that as good.

They clamor for my plays
at the Globe, pay me my price,
promise me even a share in the takings.

Fame's a surfeit of sugar tit —

Adieu, then, sonnets, Southampton,
my capricious, fickle love.

I cannot stomach ambition longer,
have sickened and soured on it.

My body craves meat.

*Playing at the Globe Theatre
through the End of the Winter Season!*

Shillings and Pence

So full of briars is this workaday world...

Principal Players

Samuel Gilbourne, apprentice

Will Slye, hireling

Philip Henslowe, rival theatre manager

Mary Burbage, sister to the Burbage brothers

Anne Phillips, wife of Augustine Phillips, actor

Cuthbert Burbage, theatre manager

William Shakespeare, actor, playwright

Anne Hathaway, Shakespeare's wife

Apprenticed

SAMUEL GILBOURNE, APPRENTICE:
The nights when we troop
gay and lively
into the Mermaid
after a long day onstage,.

the ones where fog closes,
a curtain over puddled streets,

that's when memory teases:
a familiar itch, buried
unreachable, in the small of a back.

All I'd left of home
was my father's clasp
on my small hand
as we walked the cobbles,

then he let me go.

Master Phillips,
though smiling,
bade me sing,
what was that song he taught me?

Follow follow follow follow
follow follow
follow me

How shocking
to be made to sing
so suddenly! In public,
with sodden sots
who cheer me on,
swing their tankards
at the unexpected game!

Whither should I follow follow follow
whither should I follow
follow thee?

Odd, to think how everything
trembled — voice, hands,
the very legs beneath me!
Me, who's used, now,
to the foul stench
of gawking hundreds,
mouths agape
at my most polished
melody and prance!

It was the slipping
away of my father's hand
that was hard.

The release, almost careless,
casting me forth
into the world.

I'll raise a tankard, tonight,
to my good master,
toast all the songs he's taught:

whither should I follow
follow thee?

Confession

WILL SLYE, HIRED ACTOR:
   It was the clothes I loved,
   a woman's skirts against my ankles,
   a veil draped down my back.

   More than my voice broke
   the day they made me play servant
   instead of Queen —

   me eyeing not women
   in the audience
   but our own boys,
   slender in silks,
   pirouetting about the stage,
   batting eyelashes,
   curtseying
   with flirtatious grace,

   filling me with wild,
   wanton warmth,
   making me hard.

   The bottle got me through
   those fevered nights
   drinking in alleyways
   where I'd meet others —

furtive meetings
groping in darkness,
sick the next day
with disgust —

reaching for the bottle
tilting back fluid warmth —

a warmth easier got than a man:
easier held onto, easier bought.

Henslowe's Diary

WILL SLYE, HIRED ACTOR:

Look at Henslowe
drinking with his fellows,
bloody book half falling
from his breeches' pocket
wherein lies the sum recorded
for which I am, perhaps,
damned to eternal hell.

He caught me,
like so many others,
coney in his trap,
lay in wait for me
when I was ripe
with sack and gambling,
losing at the bones,
throwing myself to perdition.

As we rose, next morning,
groaning at the winking sun,
he was all smiles, like Lucifer
in poor Marlowe's tale of that professor
who sold his soul for wealth,
summoned up devil himself,

as did I, taking money from his purse,
shining guineas so enticing
I could not stop my hand
from grasping them —

the charges' minimal, he said.

I inscribed my name
in his little diary;
spied Will Kempe there,
yes, and Ben Jonson,
and other names of my acquaintance —
felt, somehow, safer for their company,
were they not still walking,
still smiling?
Henslowe could not be as bad
as tales I'd heard,
bogey man of London —

he pointed to rough edges here and there,
torn pages in his book —
when you've paid me back,
my dear Slye, I'll hand you the page —
if you cannot, well,
we'll come to some accommodation.

All my work, day and night,
go to fill that damn usurer's purse —
he winks at me if I drink too many,

says, *remember, due day is next Monday,*
my dear man, keep paying me the interest.
I have your name here, see —
recorded in my little book.

Daybreak

MARY BURBAGE:
    and in the garden
    the apprentices practice
    falling from trees

    the older boys
    make them practice
    drill them
    cuff them when
    they will not learn

    the scullery maid
    lays out wooden trenchers
    around an ample board

    the sun rises, a hot
    scalding orange disk,
    a lark sings,

    the boys' task simple,
    preordained:

    their bones are supple

    teach them to fall now
    before they break

Care and Feeding of Apprentices

ANNE PHILLIPS, WIFE OF AUGUSTINE
PHILLIPS, ACTOR:

1.

From her hus-wife's book
Apprentices are spend-thrifts
who bear careful watching.
Do not overfeed.

2.

From a note to her cook
Last week too many bottles of ale gone;
the supply of tallow candles dwindles
dreadfully. 'Twill benefit you
to spend the evening hours
in solitude, in reflection,
not gossiping with the neighbor's cooke.
Early abed is the best rule.

3.

From a note to her husband
When does Heminge take on
another boy? Too much
of the burden of apprentices
is thrust upon our shoulders.

Ask for a bigger share of the takings
if he and Kempe do not house
another lad this season.

4.
From her hus-wife's book
Boys having trapped a rabbit this even',
I cleaned it, cubed it for a stewe.
Much stale bread, wilted onions,
sprouting potatoes eked it out —
a fine meal for all.
For once, no complaining
at the board.

Horseshoe Alley

MARY BURBAGE:

Head aching, milk heavy
in her breasts,
Mistress Phillips rises,
calls for her babe, who,
fractious, won't latch on.

Mistress Phillips lets down
her milk. A wet white puddle
floods her cotton shift.

Like a conjurer's magic,
the whisper goes through
the courtyard — stay out of sight.

The boys wish it were their week
to practice at the Heminge house,
where Mistress Heminge
feeds them bowls of oatmeal,
cuffs them, teases, sews their hose,

or even at Condell's,
where young Mistress Betsy
prays in corners,

heavy with fifth spawn —
lets the boys feed,
amply haphazard, from the pantry,

or their week at Kempe's,
where their friend the Clown
teaches them to juggle,
slip on nothing, make faces
behind the backs of tragedy —

but this is only Tuesday! The boys groan,
tighten their belts, count their pennies,

not quite sure when or where
they'll get their next good meal.

Gambling Fever

WILL SLYE:

The white heat of it!
Watching the bones fall,
their heft, their tickle in my palm
as I shift them, blow on them,
will them to do my bidding.
My heart pounds in those seconds
before they fall, obedient or defiant,

no moment in life like those few seconds,
everything more intense — smoke
from the fire, taste of the ale,
laughter of good fellows —
then narrowing in to the green baize,
watching dice roll,
click, settle back
on themselves.

Those few seconds! I forget
how I missed payment
to that devil Henslowe this week,
how I limp, buggered
too rough in the alley last night,
how that bastard Cuthbert Burbage
threatened to hold back my pay

for coming late, being ripe with sack,
missing a few tedious lines, here and there.

But I need money! Without it,
there's no drink, no dice,
no swooning under the hands of a strong man

(and, besides, Henslowe's threatened
to cut off my balls,
has ruffians who'd do it — take pleasure in it, too).

Why won't the devil dice fall my way?
My few coins dwindle, leaving me
to pant for the white heat
and the bones.

Mary, Mary

CUTHBERT BURBAGE:

    What ails you, sister? Why still single?
    One would think you pock-marked
    or sloe-faced, where instead —
    you be fair enough.

    'Tis not for lack of suitors:
    I've seen men buzzing
    about you, in ones and twos,
    men who know you've much
    to dower them, a Burbage,
    daughter of the Globe Theatre,
    well able for a household,
    sweet, smiling, kind —

    so, what prevents you?
    Father should have married you off,
    had offers for you, at twelve,
    but then you tended to him,
    so I suppose 'twas comfortable
    for you both —

well, no longer.
I can't keep you, not forever,
not even past next summer.
Haste to find you a husband, girl,
or I promise to choose you one
on my own.

Unrequited Love for Will Shakespeare

MARY BURBAGE:

As much your creature
as any of your heroines born
full-grown from your brain —

I hear echoes of my longing
in their speech,

feel the lonely wind
through my open window,

want to clamber forth,
rob my kin and yours,
hand you a dowry of devotion.

I speak to you,
blushing and unblushing,
will not die of my love,
though I do love you —
yes, with a love,
quiet and unannounced —

a love born to be scorned, perhaps,
by those women you create,
who caper onstage
bold as any boy,

who dare to love
so open, so unafraid,

so unlike me, who love
and who will die, true,
but for my love, by the Lord, no —

my love not your Sun but your Moon,
casting only the faintest of shadows
where you chose to walk.

Quite Contrary

WILLIAM SHAKESPEARE:
    She speaks to me,
    blushing and unblushing,
    brushes against me
    when there is room to spare.

    I've caught her, once, twice,
    studying my pages,
    reading raptly, her eyes half shuttered,
    rosy, to the very fingertips.

    No man alive
    could resist that flutter
    and not be flattered,

    but she is sister to the men
    I am most loyal to, in all this world,
    and I am, cruelly, married to one,

    still yearning for another.

    There's no place here for young Mary
    and her sweet, sad, untasted lips.

Avon Haystacks, Remembered Again

WILLIAM SHAKESPEARE:
Once our limbs grew weary
of love's posturings, our mouths,
employed before in silent conversation,
moving across a body
more marvelous than one's own,

opened to speech. Strange how love
provokes deeper ambitions briefly,
before sleep claims them
in sublime submersion —

how sleep, coming jointly,
made us think our dreams
were also shared in common —

but after love,
threads of conversation
return to haunt years later.
With me, sixteen,
it was being elsewhere —
it hardly mattered where —
the world opening
in all its ordinary ways —

a door deliberately unlatched,
nectar packed for travel on the well-met bee,
an oyster with its pearl peeking outward.

Anne's dreams, to spite mine,
were more domestic,
set within a farm, a family,
a world secure and closed —

and though she admired
my thrust of ambition,
I've learned her murmurs
after love were a spider web
flattering the trapped insect,
its gaze of total attention
to every furry limb.

When the bells of death do Sing

A song of death and despair, sad memories
and lives extinguished before their time.

Principal Players

Mary Burbage, sister of the Burbage brothers
Alexander Cooke, apprentice
Samuel Gilbourne, apprentice
Poor dying Tim
Anne Phillips, wife of Augustine Phillips, actor
William Shakespeare, playwright
Hamnet Shakespeare, too early dead and long mourned

Also featuring

The City Fathers
Cuthbert Burbage, theatre manager

Every Sunday

MARY BURBAGE:

We bow before the liturgy:
Almighty God, giver of all
our grace. In the pulpit,
the preacher spews forth
his sermon, taking form,
this week, as last,
on the evils of us players.

Cuthbert frowns, jiggles
his hand in his breeches pocket
as if to signify who paid,
generously, for the steeple face.

Fire and brimstone
flies from the preacher's mouth:
visitations of the devil
in the form of plague,
witchcraft, misshapen babes.

In the back, a woman cries.
She's cast forth three already
in blood and pus,
is carrying low.

Her husband helps her rise.
She makes the sign
to ward off the evil eye
moving swiftly past our pew.

I sink lower in my seat.
The preacher smiles
above his broad,
Puritan collar,
calls for a hymn.

Bear Baiting

ALEXANDER COOKE & SAMUEL GILBOURNE,
APPRENTICES:

The breath of beasts!
The ravenous mouths
gape, call for blood,
sniff the air, moan
at the missed blow,
raised arm, heavy feel
of metal upon flesh,
thin weal of the whip,
raised hackles,
smell of piss, shit,
blood puddling
on matted grass.

The crowds roar
as dog fangs split
the mass of bear,
beast gored,
innards pouring out!
A squeamish apprentice
vomits a pint of ale
and a meat pasty
on the splintered seat
before him.

Alex clutches
Samuel's goose-pocked arm,
his eyes shuttered
in sheer ecstasy.
Blood. His head sings
with it. Blood.

By Order of the City of London

1.

Pray for our souls, souls of all our citizens —
plague has struck the neighborhoods
infection spilling on our streets:

no one may congregate
in large gatherings save Church —
no bear baiting, gambling, playacting,
no assemblies for purposes other than prayer —
this applies, too, to taverns and ale houses,
all now closed by order of the City.

2.

Citizens to avoid the infected —
contagion spreads through miasmic clouds:
our dead breathe death.

Bodies to be buried together, limed and burnt
some distance from our City
(and any burying their fevered servants
within our precincts —
as our rich reported do — will be fined or worse)

the stores of unicorn horn depleted,
all houses should be strewn daily
with fresh straw or flowering boughs,
excrement contained within a corner of an alley.

3.
Vagabonds, vagrants,
all sleeping in ditches or on street corners
we deny entry to our gates,
all those with buboes or plague sores
shall be whipped and chained.

Good men should avoid prisons,
the marketplace, bawdy houses,
any place with crowds:

all this by Order of the Privy Council,
who prays for our beloved City
and all pious, God-fearing men.

Sudden Fever

MARY BURBAGE:

All night I bring him water
boiled on the hob — poor Tim
cries for his mamma, hangs
on my arm, crying, crying.

The Lord is my shepherd
hush, now, hush

I look for fever blisters,
take his wasted arms,
look under shoulders
into rank armpits,

it's there, Becky Heminge said,
you'll see the first buboe —
there, or in the groin —

he cries when I touch him,

shh, He maketh me lie down
in green pastures,
think of them, soft, green pastures
in the spring, shush...

Will there be flowers, mistress?
Daffy-down-dillies? Hey nonny no
lilies? Ah, pretty springtime lilies…

in his delirium, he sings,
in a cracked, parched voice:

    In springtime, in springtime,
      in springtime, the only pretty ring time

cries for the lute, the tambour.
The other boys hear
through the floorboards,
where I told them to stay,
safe, downstairs,

bring out their instruments
and sing — ah, good boys!

               Hey nonny no!
          Men are fools that wish to die!

Tim smiles, marking time
on his pillow
the way he's been taught,

Is't not fine to dance and sing
when the bells of death do ring?
Hey nonny no!

his hand moves, feebly, feebly,
red eyes droop,

but his voice, a thread,
spins on, a thin, foul grasp on life:

When the birds do sing, hey ding a ding a ding
hey ding a ding, hey ding a ding a ding

weakening, as I watch,
his hand slips down, eyes close.

In a moment, I'll call Cuthbert
to carry his body away,
sweep out the old straw,
strew the room with boughs.

The boys downstairs sing,
as I weep, a little, for the poor lost life.

Care and Feeding of Apprentices

ANNE PHILLIPS:

5.

From the flyleaf of her daily Bible:
Lord I beseech you
let not pestilence or plague
visit this house
let the takings be enough
to feed the boys and provide
shelter, clothes, warmth
make no inroads into my private store
let no one uncover
the clothes I've laid up for my babe
when she comes to marry
keep us free of fire, also,
and of famine
and of war

Remembering Hamnet

WILLIAM SHAKESPEARE:

I remember that day by the stream,
his warm baby breath bathing
my fond fatherly face,
Hamnet laughing as we wrestled,

then his high-toned tootling
from a tiny whistle I'd carved —
shaping his sweetness on the summer air.

"Give us your dead"
floats by tonight in London streets,
keeping time with a laden wagon
dragged past a miasma of fever,

then the dirge beyond
my neighbor's chalked door,
his cracked voice crying, *What,*
all my children? All?
All gone from me in a single night?

The church bells toll, doleful,
for him, and for me, too,

the whistle where baby lips pursed
grieving tuneless in my pocket.

On the Road to Stratford

WILLIAM SHAKESPEARE:

My mouth parched
by the road from Londontown,
the innkeeper turns on me,
sudden, and demands:
have you buried anyone of late?

I mention sad Tim not,
fearing sleep in an open field.

Poor Mary was subdued
when I stopped to say
I'd be off home
through summer's sick season,
though, truth to say,
she had reason beyond my leaving:

Tim dead, a second lad ill,
herself a maid without blemish,
but who knows when the plague hand
might strike that sweet face?

Mouthing tastelessly these hasty slops,
I miss Mary's extra helpings,
mutton and cheese,

then conjure me the table Anne will set,
a'twitter, I hope, to have me
acquiesce so unexpected to her pleading.

I'll give my love of her and the girls claim,
rather than spoiling surprise
by saying 'twas fevered London
brought me home
to write the summer time away.

Countryside Tour to Escape Plague

Here, they live filthy for years
no bathing no washing
at the sink not even a
sluice under the garden pail,

rise with the sun,
head to the fields or the shop,
hours with head bent
in prayer, talismans
keep off the evil eye,
the scourge of plague,

cut food piled lukewarm
into a trencher,
add ginger, salt, pepper,
brush maggots away,

bring animals inside,
their hot breath pants upon your cheek,
in sleep the scrabble
of rats delicate across your feet,

tell bawdy tales in near darkness,
a tallow candle

flickers, shadows deep —
frightful, alluring —
sex grasping amid a pig-pile,
the family learns not to look.

Forget the splendor,
the glamor and the thick ropes
of pearls about that neck —
she and her friends live high,
isolated, well fed but still dirty,
cold, and they stink

stink so they dull the sense
and go on vivid
with a full-throated roar.

The Lord Chamberlain's Men Present

Love in the Wrong Corners

A tale of love and longing gone astray, with everyone ending up with the wrong partner!

w i t h . . .

Anne Hathaway, William Shakespeare's wife

William Shakespeare, playwright

The Mysterious, Sensuous Dark Lady

Mary Burbage, sister to the Burbage brothers

Anne Phillips, wife of Augustine Phillips, Sharer

Will Slye, Globe Theatre hireling

Cuthbert Burbage, theatre manager

Alexander Cooke, apprentice

Back at the Globe Theatre
after a triumphant tour through the countryside!

Anne's Further Complaints

FROM A LETTER BY ANNE HATHAWAY TO
WILLIAM SHAKESPEARE:

The geese left Stratford yesterday,
honking, a long, straggling wedge
rising over the river.

They made me think of you,
husband, far again from home,
seeking some kindling of warmth
you don't find here.

Susanna had a boil
on her heel — we lanced it
at the barber-surgeon's —
you would have shuddered
to see the mess of yellow clotting
that spurt out.

Judith boiled turnip for our supper,
baked two loaves of black bread.
Going into winter, we are careful
to eat nothing but what we can trade or buy.

Your father's had trouble, again,
with the alderman and the town council.
It's not pleasant, now, to visit market.

Send me your doublet.
I'll sew the rip you wrote about,
though from what I'm told, you might find
another chit to mend your suits,
make your dinner,

even, they tell me, to warm your bed,
though I choose to dismiss idle prattle,
trusting to you, my distant gander,
to arrange matters so 'tis not true.

Care and Feeding of Apprentices

ANNE PHILLIPS:

6.

Laundry list
Sam G's doublet needs repair —
he complains 'tis tight, but the hem
will serve him yet another year,

Tim's small clothes will fit
young Nick, and he can have Sam's.

Wood ash in the soap
makes the boiled lard go further.

7.

From a note to Rebecca Heminge
Becky:
You sent me the boys last week
for meals three times, which I perforce fed them.
I cannot this week again, no matter
'tis our time or no. I send them back
and hope next time they come you'll give them
bread for my poor larder.

Counting the Coins I Do Not Have

WILL SLYE:

> Last night, Anne Phillips caught me
> counting coins out of an empty pocket,
> laughed and whispered,
>
> *Burbage is your answer,*
> *Will Slye, my fine old lad,*
>
> caught me by the elbow,
> brought me to a corner,
> bade me hush, listen.
>
> From the little office
> where old Cuthbert mumbles
> over pennies, he scolded nimble Mary,
> something about a husband,
> that she'd not live long a spinster,
> a care under his roof.
>
> Anne winked wide, circled thumb
> against her fingers,
> faded away, nodding wisely
> at my gaping grin.

So today, where Mary is,
you find Slye also —
watching her put her hand
to everything, laugh merry
at the lads, bustle about.

(If I've calculated carefully —
as I'm certain skinty Anne Phillips has —
there should be enough
dowry to settle Henslowe,
leave some over for a carouse,
any time I've a mind to one.)

I'll sound out old Cuthbert now.

I've no hankering for female flesh,
but Mistress Slye will smart for it,
if she tells her brothers
I'm a laggard
in the marriage bed.

Discoveries

MARY BURBAGE:

    Oh sweet Jesus, he knows!
    Yesterday Lark caught me
    rifling his papers, smiled slow,
    making the world turn
    upside down,
    my breath come panting,
    and asked me what I thought.

    Why should he care?
    His kindness more unkind
    than indifference, oh Lord,
    and how I muttered something
    indistinct and foolish,
    backing away from his questing hand.

    Today, his eye seeks mine in every corner,
    and when I turn from him,
    collide into Will Slye, who smiles
    as though he'd swallowed honey,
    asks if he can help me carry
    or run an errand for me, as if…

    oh Jesu, no, not that.

New Place

FROM A LETTER TO ANNE HATHAWAY
FROM WILLIAM SHAKESPEARE IN LONDON:

Indeed, indeed, Anne, you have named it well
for it will be a New Place for us to begin again.

I like it much that it is timber-framed,
spacious with five gables,
that it holds much land,
that the Avon flows beneath
— on its banks we'll bill and coo, my loyal wife,
as though we were again young lovers
and I will bring you Marlowe's flowered kirtle
and speak of him, aye, and of Ben Jonson
and the other playwrights, brave souls,
and of my fellow actors,
many fine tales, tales like good wine,
better for having waited,
dusty, in the bottle, for our imbibing.

You write the Cloptons have left the house
furnished with fine hangings, that the house
looks upon Guild Chapel — we'll walk proudly,
arm in arm, my dear, with Judith and Susanna,
across the street for prayers —

for it will be a New Place
for our girls as well, sweet Anne.

Save for me, my wife,
a space to hang our coat of arms
above the mantle — for are we not, ourselves, now,
*not without right**
— thought you it would be so, my dear,
when you urged me stay
and be a farmer with your father,
or a glover with mine? Nay,
no more of the old argument, I know you are proud
of my poor adventures, which I will tire you out
with telling, soon enough.

Soon, Anne. But now I must return
my weary pen to work, for there's a play
or two yet within me. Kiss my girls
and tend to our sweet home,

our New Place, well named, Anne — well named.

From Shakespeare's coat of arms, whose motto read "Non sans droit," (not without right).

Betrothal

MARY BURBAGE:

Will Shakespeare has left
to inspect this grand new home
his wife holds for him safe,
the place that will make him
the gentleman he longs to be.

I could not give him that,
no, nor the passion of his nights
with his noble mistress,
I am merely Mary,
the one who came too late,
unwanted, unloved.

My brother would
have me wed Slye,
make a home
within his arms.

I know not much of him,
save Cuthbert's mutterings
at the dinner table.

Can I walk into this eyes open?
Is the trap so well baited
I must fall onto the spike?

Battle of the Wills

When two Wills will battle over center stage, which Will will win?

Principal Players

William Shakespeare, *playright*

Alexander Cooke, *apprentice*

Nicholas Cooke, *apprentice*

Will Kempe, *clown*

Henry Southampton, *Earl of Wriothesley*

Cuthbert Burbage, *theatre manager*

also featuring

The Master of Revels

Servant to the Master of Revels

Elizabeth, *Queen of England*

Richard Burbage, *leading man*

John Heminge, *actor*

His Honor, the Lord Mayor of England

The Queen's Delegate

Tom Slye, *taborer*

The boys of Stratford schoolyard

Clown Disrobing

WILL KEMPE, COMPANY CLOWN:

Out of my pockets I bring such oddments
as I am known for. The rude discardings
of nobler folk — silver bells, paper cuttings,
small boxes, dolls, the odd boot.

My suit of motley, torn in spots,
marks me as clown, as rustic, as yokel.
In truth, I've never wanted another part,

for what is life but all too full of tragedy,
and wherefore should we waste sweet daylight
putting pain for fools to gape at on the stage?

Nay, they're better off with me, Chief Fool,
bumpkin and rudesby, my feet decked
in extra large shoes,
that I lean forward now to unlace,

kick off into the corner for my little cur to gnaw.
He and I understand our place,
look separate for our bones —
I feed him meat and sinew after my own reward:
applause, applause and melodious laughter.

Like Lucifer (that old Beelzebub,
my eternal fellow prankster),
I understand that laughter is but
the other side of agony
— there's no ribaldry without the joke's butt,
someone must needs serve as reverse to contentment,
the one who moans
when others hold their sides with mirth.

Bed is a warm fellow, we'll be better acquainted
before dawn. I gather up my clown's trappings,
give them a good shove into a corner,
blow out candle, drape myself with quilted cover,
huddle down to dream
of new counterfeits and tricks.

The Whore, Our Play

RICHARD BURBAGE:

'Tis hardest for our playwright,
his work naked before the censor,
flaunting itself like some whore
bent over a polished table.

The Master of Revels suffers from toothache
today — so his servant whispers, scuttling about
— his temper's sharp as a baited bear.

The Master sips from a flagon of warmed mead
flavored with spice meant to numb the senses,

which, by the pained look on Shakespeare's face,
has bypassed gums, gone straight to brains,
fogging them, as the Master excises
choice passages, changes words,
cuts, makes Shakespeare wince,

then smile widely, falsely.

A long afternoon wears on —
by its end, the whore, our play,
leaves behind a treasured drape or two,
is sore in her nether limbs,
limps, mayhap, over some ravaged passages,

but struts nonetheless, the ravine
between her dugs a gold mine,
paying us a year's wages
for a light skirt and
a single night's revelry.

Before Her Majesty

NICHOLAS TOOLEY, APPRENTICE:

1.

I'd heard tales
of earlier apprentices
dragged off, to face
the wheel, the tongs,
the red hot poker's tip —

so the first time I played
for good Queen Bess.
I lay sleepless half the night before,

pictured her as giantess,
striking death
from a commanding hand,

thought of being clapped in irons
for the certain crime of misspoke lines.

2.

Brought to the antechambers
to prepare, I could smell
roast pork, rich waftings
of small partridge, even more
exotic scents. Alex Cooke
said 'twas the smell

of roasting servant boy —
nothing the Queen
liked better, unless it be
boiled apprentice.

3.
The beauty of the Queen's rooms
will furnish my dreams 'til death!

Thick carpets,
hangings made from gold,
immense portraits of royals
and their loyal dogs!

My brothers and sisters would stare
to see me supping
from a board so long it groaned

drinking cider with a faint
aroma of the East, eating dainty
milk pudding dusted sweet.

4.

The Queen turned out
nothing more
than a wizened thing
hung with pearls
in a big red wig.

I liked her.

She winked at me as I bent
to pet her dog,
turned back easy and smiling,
to command our scribbler, Will:

Give me another play
with Falstaff — that braggart
makes me laugh,

affable, nodding toward our clown,
Will Kempe, who grinned
and danced and bowed.

Overheard, 1: Will Kempe

WILL KEMPE:

Piss on all
playwrights,
especially those
called Will.

Their tragedies not
for such as me!
I'll have my cake and ale,
reread the play,

discover where
laughs are needed,

instruct my feet
to dance a jig,
a morris, mayhap,
make them laugh
and cry fie,
fie on tragedy!
Thumb my nose
at Will —
have my will
the only will
regarded.

୨

Popularity

WILLIAM SHAKESPEARE:

See Kempe there,
cup brimming,
mouth ambling non-stop —
laughing, mugging, mocking.

The boys love him the way
they adore a hefty meal,
with sweetmeats at its end —

why, he's nothing more
than trifle to them
— rum-soaked cake
half-collapsed under
a heavy pile of nuts,
fruit, cream —
and being boys, they dig in,
knowing full well by midnight
they'll be rolling in agonies
regretting their half-digested gorging —

'tis useless, I suppose, to say
that I have never been adverse to his tricks
even when they have hurt me most.

My fellow actors roll their eyes at my complaints,
see Kempe as nothing more harmful than trifle
— don't see the chaos panting underneath,
how unchecked mirth, left unbalanced,
can serve to topple us all.

Southampton at the Globe

WILLIAM SHAKESPEARE:

1.

I knew 'twas he,
his sweet breath
on my unsuspecting neck,
all smiles at my wide eyes,
delight leaping
as I turn blithely to his wit:

> *You look well, Will,*
> *decked in Friar's robes.*

Smiling on me,
all powder and scent,
a ruff so high
he can barely turn his head.

> *Your fellows have taken good care of me,*
> *seated me upon the stage with my party*
> *— 'tis My Lord Essex,*
> *see, there, and the two Percys.*

(The noble company
turn at his mention,
bow and smile.)

We're all agog to see your play,
my good Bard.
'Tis too long since
you've honored my halls.
Come tonight as celebration?

I nod,
all force and joy,
my bobbing like that
of My Lord's favorite hound,
tail wagging

but I cannot help myself,
no, nor help the growling whisper,
the faintest croak stripping
my throat as I lean
toward His Lordship:
And she?

Just that ill-conceived moment,
Dick Burbage pulls me away,
questioning a scene,
forcing me to wait and wonder.

2.

I watch him, undetected
— I hope — from behind the arras,
my blood hot, my breath
rasping in my ears —
to see if my play pleasures him,
more tender of his judgment
than before Her Majesty,
it seems vital, in that moment,
my words, my words alone,
must make him smile, frown —

3.

Mid-way, he dispatches a message,
writ on hot-pressed paper, which I unfold,
awkward as the schoolgirl
I'd written about onstage:

Will, your play moves me more than I can speak!
Who dares say our playwrights cannot match
those of antique Rome or Athens — my fellow,
you have done it this day! I fair burst
with pride in the beauty unfolding, and she will, too,
for I will help you stage this for her,
and she will fall, ripe fruit, into your hands again.

4.

I speak my lines, distracted
by his beaming face so close,
at dinner, I will tell him
of my fine country house,
he'll draw me back into his golden circle

and she'll be there, tonight,
or if not tonight, then soon.

5.

Then Kempe bursts forth
upon the play, tromps onstage,
swilling lines, jostling lads,
mugging, acting the buffoon,
who, hat in hand, seeks pennies
for the pratfall.

My face an ice storm, froze horror
— Kempe juggles my tragedy,
conjures it into mum-show,
all for a shallowness of cheering,
the roaring of groundlings.

My Lord sits there dejected,
biting a finger, shrugging,
pointing off at me.

Kempe whirls back,
grinning at the destruction,
brushes past me,
all hot and steaming.

6.
Afterward, the excuse,
written shamefaced,
delivered by a red-caped page:

> *Shakespeare, many apologies*
> *My Lord Essex commands my presence*
> *tonight, and then I'm off*
> *on travels, but much moved, still,*
> *by your tragedy.*

A tragedy, yes, of classic proportions.
But of Romeo and Juliet,
perhaps not, not today,
or perhaps not only.

◈

Overhead, 2: Will Shakespeare

WILLIAM SHAKESPEARE:

There's nothing for it.

Anne didn't write,
not today, not yesterday,

but her grief
for our Hamnet
walks the miles between us.

Cuthbert clamors
for yet another play:
won't see that I'm wearing thin,
invention spitting slower
off the quill.

Kempe eyes me black,
wants to crown me
with a motley cap.

My lover left me,
while I was sweet asleep.
Took sonnets as her booty,
left me, a ruined man.

Now I write plays for groundlings,
a rowdy commerce on the brutish stage,

a travesty of the poet
I wanted to become,

the poet I still feel within me.

Final Provocation

WILLIAM SHAKESPEARE:

That varlet, prattle-witted,
swollen dropsy-laden bag
of vanity — send him forth,
or I take me and my plays
and find employ with Henslowe!

Cuthbert, you saw him,
egging on the lads,
teaching them tricks like a mutt
her pups! His wayward pranks
made mockery of my lines,
ripped the bleeding heart from my play,
turned it upside down, gave it a fine shake,
tore it to tatters, to rags!

Each day this week, he's held court
on stage — court jester, only artless
and ill-meaning, with malice, jarring
the muse of Tragedy aside,
elbowing out my poor lovers,
for the gaping, gawking, grinning groundlings,
that popinjay, that wit-lackey,
that folly-fallen malady!

I say it one more time, Cuthbert!
Henslowe knows what's toward,
has spoke to me of fattening my purse
to write for him — I want none of him,
understand, but I want none of Kempe
and his rank parade of mockery, either!

Have him step one more jarring foot upon the stage,
and you'll see my back, for good and all!

Speak the Speech

WILLIAM
SHAKESPEARE:

And let those that play
your clowns speak
no more than is
set down for them;

WILLIAM
KEMPE:

Curse me, all I did
was deviate from
the deadliest of lines —
lines requiring a midwife
to twist them, so aborted
the stage reeked
of the afterbirth.

Did you hear
the audience roar?
Who is this Shakespeare
to think they are nothing
more than poppets, jointed
manikins, mouths open
only on command?

for there be of them
that will
themselves laugh,
to set on
some quantity of
barren spectators
to laugh too;

What are we there for
but to please them,
glad they plopped
their penny in our box?
That penny as good as one
from nobleman
or university professor,
easier to please, predictable,

without brains fermenting
a discarded onion in the sun.

though,
in the mean time,
some necessary question
of the play be then
to be considered:

Question of the play, paugh!

Do we play with pokers
up our asses — marbles
in our mouths?
What questions
can a play ask?
Mouthings about man's
place, God's glory, destiny,
fate, good, evil...
it makes the head spin.

Give me instead
an honest laugh,
a good scratch of the balls
at day's end, provoke the
two-headed beast to make
more mouths to ope
in merriment,

growth of audience
more natural than

straining at meaning,
undigested fodder
lumpy in our stool.

That's villainous,
and shows
a most pitiful ambition
in the fool
that uses it.

What odds ambition,
Shakespeare?

You with your crest of arms,
shoulder rubbing with
Southampton,
willing pander to our good
Queen Bess...

My fellow actors, think
before you act,
become naught but worse
than dumb show,
transformed to asses,
beasts of burden capable
of nothing but carrying only
his precious speeches —

and consider how history
will regard *you*, elbowing *me*
aside to gratify his conceit.

Leavetaking

WILL KEMPE:

In truth, I say farewell
with a light heart!
I will not miss early
mornings, boys tugging
my sleeves, begging
another lesson gamboling,
juggling, tumbling, prancing about.
Nor being pricked by dresser's needle,
prosed to by bookman,
enduring rehearsals
where Burbage drops his cues,
Heminge struts about, fat peacock,
Will Shakerag moans the brutal misuse
of his precious turds of prose.

Gad, 'tis a wonder
I endured it all this time!

Those lengthy afternoons
hunched behind a doorway, waiting
for a break in their dreary speeches
to lighten the stage an instant
with my enchantment — hard to believe
I kept my patience and good temper
these many years! Nay, I'll not miss them,

and their petty quarrels, tussles over
pocket change, wailing at trifles!
They've seen my back —
now let them beg — seeing Her Majesty has written
to signify her joy of my morris dance,
His Honor the Lord Mayor's summoned me
to stay at his own house,
break fast with him the day of my departure!

What need I of the Globe's players,
their wretched airs and tragic graces?
They'll rue their decision soon enough —
much may it profit them!

Morris Morning

WILL KEMPE:

1.

His Lordship the Mayor
gave me a soft feather bed
to sleep in, but even it
couldn't damp down my doubts
as I tossed and turned — ah! but
in comfort.

It's cold out, colder than I'd wagered on.

The board's set for two hundred citizens,
all here to drink an early morning tankard
and wave me off on my morris dance
from London to Norwich —

her Majesty the Queen dispatched a delegate,
I hear, some pretty lordling in a velvet cap.

Come! Stop this frowsing, Will Kempe,
sluice some water on your pallid countenance,
paste a smile on your vapid face!

2.

The crowd's bigger than I thought
'twould be — there I see the Globe boys

waving their arms frantic — ah, good lads,
good lads — I miss them, sometimes,
more than might have been supposed.

Tom Slye my taborer straps drum
across one shoulder, smiles over it,
awaits my signal to begin.

A slip now, on this icy patch,
will start them roaring — ow! as did it,
'tis easy, always, to snare
a crowd's fickle love.

Now up and frolic, William Kempe,
show them a wonder they'll talk of
many years after they forget

(*one two, one two*)

some others who preen themselves
and their lines so important,
one can't interrupt them
with so much as a fart.

3.
The crowds waning, finally
at the outskirts of London,
the pathways hard caked mud.

Onward, Will! *(one two)*

here's the first farmyard —
make the ploughboy,
milkmaids love you, dance
and skip, stumble, fall,
laugh. Laugh!

Shakerags

WILL SHAKESPEARE:

Old Kempe in his pamphlet,
Nine Daies Wonder,
trying to mock me,
pulls out the old trick —

my dreadful, common name:
Shakespeare.

Nothing new, of course —
since my gran'fer Richard
was called once
Shakstaff
by a faulty scribe —

the boys in Stratford
schoolyard full of

Shaxper
Shagspere
Wagspere
Waggestaff

Extravagant christeners,
they'd call out
Breake-speare
when I farted

Shot-bolt
when I'd run for cover

Strong-shield
for enduring
master's thrashing

one in particular
tried out
Wiggle-worm,
lewdly gesticulating
as if mine were
a minor manhood

good training, all of it,
first for Greene,
my friend of the Upstart Crowe
who crowned me Shake-scene
in my own conceit

and now for Kempe
that dancing ninny
who calls me Shakerags

and is himself
nothing more
than unkempt
uncouth
unkind
upstaged

A favorite of Her Majesty the Queen
Now presented to the Public at the Globe Theatre

Exchange of Wills

A tale of three women and their
fascination with one man,
and what they will do
to possess him

The Mysterious Dark Lady
Mary Burbage, sister to the Burbage Brothers
Will Slye, hireling
Will Shakespeare, playwright
Anne Hathaway, Shakespeare's wife

a l s o   f e a t u r i n g
Cuthbert Burbage, Globe Theatre Manager
The Dark Lady's Servant
Katrice, the Dark Lady's Friend
Susanna Shakespeare, Shakespeare's older daughter
Judith Shakespeare, Shakespeare's younger daughter
John Hall, suitor of Susanna Shakespeare

Bridal Preparations

MARY BURBAGE:

1.

Spare no expense, Cuthbert says,
a feast to remember!

Dough rolled with citron and spices,
collops of lamb with mint sprigs,
the pig butchered and smoked —

every delicacy I store in the back pantry
feels heavy in my hands, like funeral meats.

2.

Slye is lover-like enough, brings me ribbons
for my hair, posies I prop in a glass,
offers me the wine first, holds the door,

but he is restrained —
kisses, caresses, the little touchings
between lovers he keeps to himself.

3.

Rumor has it the Dark Lady
is also betrothed; Will walks about,
face pinched, sallow.

He writes her, dispatches the letters
through Nick Tooley, who, for a penny
brings them to me first.

How can she withstand
his twisting agony, his longing?
I borrow the letters for a night,
keep them under my pillow,
whisper *Will, Will,* in solitary passion.

Were I to moan out the name
loud, piercing — no one would be the wiser,

certainly not this troth-mate,
this shadow Will,
who watches me lay up
jellies in a crimson row,
lips moving as he counts the jars.

The Letter

MARY BURBAGE:

His letter burns my hands, scalds my skin.
I feel his passion rising from the lines,
huge smoky waves of need;

if this were mine, addressed to me,
entreating me, wanting me,
I would not fail him:

> *My Company meets tonight to toast our fellow,*
> *marrying tomorrow to Mary Burbage,*
> *also of our Company,*
> *there will be much carousing: drink, song,*
> *some general gibing, jests running freely,*
> *as you would expect —*

> *my taste unfit for bridals these days*
> *I can slip away, to meet you — think of you, me,*
> *these warm June nights*
> *a few stolen hours in Southampton's gardens*

> *I will be there by midnight, love.*

The page he touched
I tuck against my breast,
all day it prickles me:

just one night I want my Will
to be the one Will I want.
I will myself courage,
my Will enthralling my night,
our night, tonight,
to the night I will,
whispering, under my breath,
intoxicated with my own Will:

Do I dare? Do I dare?

Stolen Night

WILLIAM SHAKESPEARE:

Every woman's flesh is different —
a man could become enamored
of moving from body to body,
to taste, to touch, to hold
as many different sensations
as there are women, multiplied again
by as many women's moods,
then again by the bending of their knees,
their rippling backs,
the exquisite tremor of their thighs
during penetration.

I never expected that Mary,
of all my women,
would taste most flavorful to my tongue,
that she would come to me,
rising from the evening mist as fugue,
that we would move slowly,
in a dream toward one another,
that our hands would work magic,
clothes slip away as though cast by spell,
our bodies meeting, melding,
not one word spoken

not one needed.

Mary's Wedding Dress

MARY BURBAGE:

    Becky Heminge's arms are full of the dress,
    creeping worriedly into my room
    in the pearly dawn.

    She holds it up and frowns.

    It's taken on a slight pink sheen,
    from being washed
    with something red, she says.

    I smile, faintly, sadly, and put it on.

The Dark Lady's Wedding Dress

HER SERVANT SPEAKS AGAIN:

Last night my lady came to me,
tears in her dark eyes, asked me
to burn some letters in a coal hot brazier.

Her trunks are packed, corded,
addressed to his lordship's wooded estate,
where she will spend her first days
as captive as the fawns
he loves to shoot and eat.

The letters curl and burn in the fire.
I warm my hands over their slight flame.

Her bridesmaid reclines at ease
against the cushions while I lace
each pearl seed fastening
up the curve of my lady's spine.
Should I have gone, Katrice?
my lady whispers,

*Do you think he stayed
in Southampton's gardens,
all night, pining for me?*

Katrice pins the veil in her black hair.
I put a rope of pearls
about her long dun neck.

My Husband, We Are Well

FROM A LETTER TO WILL SHAKESPEARE
FROM ANNE HATHAWAY:

It has been long since you have written,
but the lengthening days cheer us,
the three beautiful women Will Shakespeare
calls his own:

Susanna, Judith, and, of course, his Anne.

I smile as I write it, Will,
for I must tell you Susanna has a beau,
a doctor, yes, we're growing old,
you and I, my dear, time to move aside,
let young ones scoop up their share of romance.

His name is John Hall, of good family,
which I know will please you, and he writes
too, on medicine, which I think
will please you.

Susanna is happy, Will — come home
this summer to see her fine glow.

Husband, I hope you are content,
but not too content —

some in Stratford gossip.
I do not heed their stories,
though sadly I admit the townspeople do,
they point at me and sneer.

Our fine new home
gives me comfort in your absence.
You will like John Hall and I take pleasure
that you will soon lose two of your women,
leaving you, my dear husband, in these,
your last, your final years

with your only devoted Anne.

A Stratford-upon-Avon production

elease Me from My Bands

Nearing the end of his life,
will shakespeare relinquishes
his own brand of magic,
and finds the world
without it bereft.
Can it be reattained
through a lost love?

P r i n c i p a l   P l a y e r s

Samuel Gilbourne, apprentice

Will Slye, hireling

Mary Slye, wife of Will Slye

William Shakespeare, retired playwright

Anne Hathaway, Shakespeare's wife

a l s o   f e a t u r i n g

Henry Southampton, Earl of Wriosley

The Earl of Essex

The rebels of the Essex Revolt

Richard Burbage, leading man

John Heminge, Sharer

Ben Jonson, playwright

And the entire King's Men cast

Old Fool After the Rebellion

WILLIAM SHAKESPEARE:

> *Give me the crown. Here, cousin, seize the crown;*
> *Here cousin:*
> *On this side my hand, and on that side yours.*
> *Now is this golden crown like a deep well*
> *That owes two buckets, filling one another,*
> *The emptier ever dancing in the air,*
> *The other down, unseen and full of water:*
> *That bucket down and full of tears am I,*
> *Drinking my griefs, whilst you mount up on high.**

I feel a fool.
My fellow players wink
at my falling in with Essex, Southampton,
joining their treachery against the crown,
rehearsing in dark corners
that hell-borne play,
that sad and censored bucket scene
once sternly outlawed.

We played the excised scene
in broad daylight,
half the watchers
ripe for any mischief,
the others thirsty for a slaking
only the red drink could quench.
Yet a day later, denied blood and glory,

London shuddering behind closed shutters,
the rebels hurried, harried, home,
lonely cobbles echoing in defeat.

I feel a fool, a failure.
There was a heady moment when,
as if young again, the thought
of putting out my hand
to shape a kingdom's throne
awakened in me ambition, greed,
that longing I am cursed with:

to be something more than what I am.

Lucky we players that
Her Most Indignant Majesty
holds a soft spot for us,
excused us with a scold,
made of my crimes no more
than scalding whisper
that London mouths as it points at me,
old fool, old failure, old man.

*Lines from Richard II, previously censored as they suggested
royalty could be deposed, which were included in a special perform-
ance to the Earl of Essex's rebels on February 7, 1601.

The King's Men

CUTHBERT BURBAGE:

Our dresser had three nights,
two days to outfit all of us.
Somehow, the uniforms are ready,
laying before us in disembodied state
in the tiring room,
the potential of pressed new clothes,
expectant upon them.

Throughout London,
cannon fire booms,
church bells ring,
people on the cobbles
shout:

The Queen is dead,
long live the King!

The Queen is dead.
We dress in scarlet cloth,
livery servants to His Majesty.

Dick and Will instruct apprentices
to behave as we march
through thronged streets,
members of the royal cavalcade,

The clock strikes.
We set out, a scarlet mass,
heads high, our dignity
fresh as new red cloth,
enobling us
in the glory of the day.

We roar, together with the crowds:
The Queen is dead.
Long live His Majesty King James!

Fire!

SAMUEL GILBOURNE, APPRENTICE:

From the stage, only waves of heat
cascade, actors stumbling mid-speech
before the groundlings, a sudden hush harsh calls
pointing fingers skyward *the thatch! the thatch!*
those at front falling back, elbowing aside
screams shouts children hoisted forgotten
smoke curling down roof above blazing
a hundred pair of boots thudding
close packed earth agonized *momma!*
cries for help for children —

we trapped onstage, flames licking arras columns
flares jumping thatch falling burning clumps
crawling through smoke haze clouds of dust
down down down ground rising up
crouched coughing, heavy phlegm clogging throat
Jesu save us! gasping grunting catching an arm
grabbed from behind half-carried out head tucked
beneath someone's heavy coat air thinning
wheezing smoke din dirt coughing choking

air! eyes rimmed weeping the entire Globe
burning Shakespeare crying Burbage sucking an arm
burnt blistered Heminge begging anyone
rescue the words the words are burning
plays costumes props consumed consumed

the words! none here. We stand, gaping, charred ruin
our limbs unmoving, black soot,
our eyes glazing, rubbed to rawness,
our mouths empty, the words we'd use now ash.

Puppeter No Longer

WILLIAM SHAKESPEARE:

I once thought, like my Prospero,
that I could shape an entire age
by my own hand,

thought to raise myself
from humble origins,
put aside that young Will
running over fields
in early mornings,
pressing a nose up
against the thick steamed glass
of a bakeshop window,

conjure myself
into someone
whose heady airs and graces
sat comfortably,
a purple mantle draped
over padded shoulders,

thought I could pipe the tune
to which my players would dance —
on stage, and off stage, too.

But I grow old.

I cannot match
these jaded bucks
for whom our brave new world
turns stale, Jacobean fops
who paint patches,
demand candlelight,
and a closed stage;

refinements we at the Globe
could not fathom, as we played
in all weathers, under the unblinking eye
of sun, before a rowdy,
adventurous, questing, simple London.

It's time, Will Bard,
pack your moldy traps,
head home to Anne.

Retirement

WILLIAM SHAKESPEARE:
That first morning, uneasy,
I awoke.

Late morning through
whorled glass
gleamed green and hot,

sounds of the kitchen
filtered up through floorboards.

I listened.
The village outside long awake,
the whir of wheels,
livestock, tradesmen
through the streets, striding

brisk, but without the acute
importance stamping the London
cobbles I'd grown used to.

A door opened and shut,
footsteps hovered
by the landing,

my family unsure what to do with me,
whether to wake me
or leave me lie in the unaccustomed
luxury of a late morning bed —

I unsure myself.
But there was the rest of life
unclaimed, ahead.

I rose, pissed, sluiced at the basin,
went down to Anne,
to Susanna,
to Judith,
to the new day.

Married Mary

MARY SLYE:

Under his drunken eye,
I've learned to move, fast, fast,
be quiet, watchful,

no longer wait for love.

The accident child has become,
herself, an accident waiting —
in a second, his fist
strikes from nowhere:

purple pain and stars
twirling dizzy what he gives me,
names like whore, slut,
pinchpenny when I hide the money
he spends on dice and drink

and men.

Cuthbert cannot meet my swollen eye,
not that I blame him — much.

'Tis well Shakespeare doesn't see me
wilting to nothing
under Slye's relentless fist.

Only calm when he's gone,
crashed out in a fury,
me crumpled, sobbing in a corner —
when I rest my throbbing head,
remember that I had, in my poor life,
one moment when my love held me close,
whispering my name
to our single summer night,
a fusing as bee-brief
as visiting a flower
in the slip of midsummer's moon,
warmth flowing through us both,

our passion fallen now,
denuded, bare, froze frost.

Boredom

WILLIAM SHAKESPEARE:

Every morning I walk for hours,
through the town,
past the schoolyard
where they teased me,
past the marketplace,
the tavern,
into the fields.

I visit hillocks and haystacks,
walk past farmers
who shake their heads at me,
an oddment: man at leisure,
puffing a pipe, during harvest hours.

Anne has her rhythm all alone,
years without me,
moves from task to task
all fluid current,
knows when to turn
the rushes on the floor,
when to visit market,
bake bread.

The people in my head persist,
angry at me that I will not
write them down.

I have to walk far, far,
tire myself by noon each day
to still their shouting,
their beating
inside my skull.

Can We Meet?

What they tell me of you
hurts me, Mary Burbage —
Burbage, I still name you,
never Slye, for the man
they matched you with deserves
not one whit of your consideration —

they say he beats you.
I wince and feel blows
as though rained upon my shoulders,

for I have that one night
kept warm and secret these many years
and am fond of it, of you,

would not make matters worse,
but, growing old and staid
and, frankly, sad,
wrinkled, bent more
with weight of years
to come than actual
counted time,

ask one last glance
of your sweet eyes
to remind me of that night,
of your love for what I once was.

Anticipation

i. MARY SLYE:

'Tis foolish to have to stop and wait
for my breath to catch up with me!
The day seems golden, a ripe pear,
finally ready to drop into my hand,
so sweet, so juicy — the first bite
explodes, eyes shut in concentrated
sense, nothing but pear, pear

pear. My hands have moved, this morning,
all without me, undirected, they folded
clothes, swept the floor, the rest of me
waiting for that first bite,
that man who floods my senses

ii. WILL SHAKESPEARE:

Anne not pleased I chose
my birthday for this journey —
but it's long since I've broke bread
with Ben Jonson, the other playwrights,
that carping, talented crew, who honor me,
elder statesman of the stage,
a gentle Homer led, blind, by the hand,
directed to the place of glory.

That's for tonight. Today, I'll meet poor Mary,
look sad upon what I am told
is a broken face, offer her, perhaps,
a little comfort, nostalgia, a final soft caress.

iii. MARY SLYE:

Dip into the cosmetics of the stage
to hide my wounded face,

select a dress from the tireman's store —
something soft about the shoulders,
with gauzed sleeve,

dress my hair with pommade and gilt
and powder — lucky I 'tis the fashion —

but will he see the rocky surface of my jowls,
creases between my eyes,
heavy spots on my dried, knobbly hands?

iv. WILL SHAKESPEARE:

One pants at the entranceway to the stage —
so unexpected this! All my years drop away,
make me remember that first afternoon
with her father, when I might

have spied a warmth
in her sweet eyes,
had I only known to look!

v. MARY SLYE:

He slides his hand across
his thinning brow,
adjusts his doublet,
looks left and right.

Sad memory tugs at me,
makes me think of us,
our lives propelled
on uncharted courses,
we two orbiting together,
twin moons about one globe,
colliding with sparks.

It could have been so.
Just so. Just so.

Rebuff

MARY BURBAGE:

    And, after all, I only wanted
    the touch of his hand,
    his smile looking past
    my ravaged face,
    solid thud of footsteps
    sounding next to mine
    as we walked by the river.

    When he moved close
    to caress me,
    I eased back
    out of his crowding arm.

    'Twas right, though I could see
    hurt in his eyes

    hurt that I thought him old, worn,
    damaged by years,
    mockery of the slender youth
    he still expected to see
    in puddled reflection,
    the lad I remember
    sliding awkwardly
    from my father's doorstep,

till courage took hold
and he knocked
and entered my life.

We could not have now
what was never meant,
I murmured, and he subsided,
face reflecting so many things:
pain, fear, sadness, relief.

He kissed me on the forehead
when he left.

I knew my life
without him
was now all left to me.

Drink Up, Lads

WILLIAM SHAKESPEARE:

The young ones drink me in
eyes all awe and wonder,
speak as though I were my own best creations —
enigmatic Hamlet, magnificent Prospero,
cunning Hal. There's a distance in their eyes,
unbridgeable, making of me more than what I am.

They pick the wrong characters
to pin to my shoulders.
Better should they consider me jealous Othello,
ambitious Macbeth, poor doddering Lear,

or even best, just me, hempseed Will Shakespeare,
son of Stratford, hailed in London for a space
for a few liked plays — sent out to pasture, now,
to the same green fields that saw my breeding.

They raise their glasses to me — *Will Shakespeare!*
Bard of Avon! Father of Theatre! Father of us all!
I drain each tankard;
some pipsqueak fills it brim full
from a pitcher handy.
Sweet William! Mellifluous poet!
Here's Ben Jonson calling out: *Soul of the Age!*
The applause! delight! The wonder of our Stage!

In time, words fall spinning — mine own, as well.
Twice do I try to find my feet to swelling applause,
a jackass braying to their clamor, interrupting:
Oh, Star of Poets! Bright light of our constellation!
A willful wit! A wonderous wit! A witfull will!
Finding my mouth empty, they laugh, pull me down
and press upon me to drink deep again.

They crowd about, faces flushed, in close quarters
to my glorious self, raising toasts, rubbing my sleeve,
fumbling my shoulder, slapping my back.

Fumes of drink cloud what little thoughts
remain. A merry band, we, elbow benders all,
good fellows, urging ourselves
to love each what we do best,
the words we pen, women we've forgotten,
little spillage of our days, wiped up,
beer splatter with a greasy cloth.

It's late, the thin rim of dawn gives false light.
There are no stars out when I stagger forth.
A sudden darkness rushes up

and in slow time I fall.

No Longer Mourn

MARY SLYE:

   The churchbell chimes.
   Its every hollow sound
   says gone, gone, gone.

   In my memory,
   a sonnet he wrote when young,
   young still, still in love:

   chiding us: forget the hand that writ.

   He never understood, I think,
   his life measured not
   in hours upon the stage,
   in crests, in titles
   or even — sadly for me,
   for Anne,
   for his dark haunting desire —
   in love,
   but measured by
   that hand that writ —
   in his words,
   or, yes, in fact, in love,
   drunk in love,
   a reeling, giddy love,

love of language,
of a peopled earth, all dancing
moving, speaking
to the sway and measure
of that hand of his that writ.

It is what is left me;
left us all:
the hand that writ
the words he wrote
the worlds he issued forth.

Breaking the Vow

MARY SLYE:

1.

Returning from Lark's gravesite,
I cannot re-enter my house.

My husband, drunk already,
sprawls inside, his hair
spilled on a table,

my hand backs from the door,
legs refuse me.

One Will is gone from me, forever,
and, standing here, unwilling,
I find I lack the will
to make a life
wedded to this shadow Will.

2.

Long ago, newly bereft of father,
we gathered mourners under Cuthbert's roof.

'Twas then my Lark proposed
to move old lumber,
set foundations in a new place.

3.

I turn down the path,
break one vow,
make one new:

to live my life as I will it,
step out from under
the shadow of the Globe
into the luminescence
of my own bright day.

Author's Note

The poems in this book comprise an interpretive biography of some aspects of William Shakespeare's life, loves, and ambitions, but, while based on historical events, this narrative is a work of fiction and, as such, does not precisely match an authentic chronology. Mary Burbage and several minor characters, including the Orange Girl, the Dark Lady's friend, Katrice, and the Dark Lady's servant were invented characters. The Dark Lady's identity remains the mystery it has been for centuries. All other individuals mentioned were, in fact, real people with documented histories, but any resemblance between their actual lives and my portrayal of them should be considered no more than astonishing good luck.

Acknowledgements

Grateful acknowledgement is made to the editors of the following publications in which these poems, some in earlier versions and with other titles, have appeared:

AtomicPetals: "Bear Baiting"
The Dakota House Review: "Countryside Tour to Escape Plague" appeared as "Recipe for Elizabethan Living"
Eclectica: "Anne's Further Complaints" appeared as "Anne Hathaway's Further Concerns"
Literary Potpourri: "Discarded" appeared as "Shakespeare Discarded"
Stirring: A Literary Collection: "Writing Romances"

Appreciation

I would like to thank early readers Ruby Riemer, William Van Buskirk, Lyn Sanders, and Theresa Serrano for their encouragement, as well as the members of the Scribblers writers group, Elaine Denholtz, Joan Morrison, Marjorie Keyishian, and Carole Rogers, who offered criticism and guidance. Susan Rothbard was the first to point out that the book needed to find a narrative shape. I owe special thanks to my two most constant readers, Stacy Coffelt and Kathy Harris, who had the patience to read several iterations. Walter Cummins offered praise of the initial manuscript and served as match-maker, recommending it to my publisher. My mentor, Sondra Gash, worked with me through countless line-by-line critiquing sessions — to Sondra, I owe gratitude and much more. Eileen Murray graced this book with her unerring sense of design. Steve Cameron, Matthew Kreps, Myfanwy Collins and Carol Peters all took great pains in copy editing. Patty Tompsky continues to work tirelessly to promote the book. I am especially grateful that Beverly Jackson, my editor and publisher, only accepted this book when it was truly ready, and had the generosity of spirit to work with me until it was. And, of course, I could never have completed this work without the unswerving, loving support of my husband, Steve, and sons Geoff and Alex, for whom I quote: *what I have done is yours; what I have to do is yours; being part in all I have, devoted yours.*

About the Author

Michelle Cameron's poetry has appeared in *The Paterson Literary Review, Literary Potpourri, Midnight Mind, Lilith, Lips, Uno, Riding the Meridian, 2River View, Samsara Quarterly, Stirring, Eclectica, AtomicPetals, The Paumanok Review,* and *flashquake,* among many others. Her poems have been selected as "Editor's Choice" in the 2002 Allen Ginsberg Contest, and Best of Stirring Year Three. She lives in New Jersey with her husband and two sons.